Late Merging

*Getting ahead
On and Off the Road*

Written and illustrated by

Jenz Johnson

© Copyright 2025 Jenz Johnson

All Rights Reserved. No part of this publication may be reproduced, stored in a retrieval system, or transmitted in any way or by any means, including photocopying, recording, or storing it in any medium by electronic means, without the written permission of the author.

Library of Congress Cataloging-in-Publication Data
Johnson, Jenz
Late Merging: Getting Ahead On and Off the Road
    pages cm

ISBN 978-0-9779586-2-7

1. Driver Education 2. Decision Making and Problem Solving. 3. Success

Birdrock Press
P.O. Box 12866
La Jolla, California 92039
www.birdrockpress.net

Founded in 2004, Birdrock Press rides a different wave with writers whose passion for their subject matter sets them apart. Birdrock Press offers special editions for academic curriculums.

Printed in the United States of America
First printing April 2025
R 24.7e

Contents

1. Introduction 1
2. Driving as an Art 5
3. Merging Basics 11
4. Hand Signals 19
5. Signs 23
6. Driving Skills 29
7. Life Skills 49
8. Quick Guide 79
9. Glossary 83
10. Endnotes 85

Preface

Dear Fellow Driver,

The idea for this book came to me while I was stuck in traffic. The stalled drivers all around me had drifted into their own worlds. One was tapping to music behind closed windows and appeared to be singing at the top of his lungs. Another was applying makeup and transforming from a sleepy mophead into a friendly store clerk. Several others were furiously texting while keeping one eye on the traffic. Every day I sat in the same logjam, just waiting---and wasting my life away.

Suddenly out of the corner of my eye, I saw a yellow Toyota slipping between the lanes ahead of me, finding openings between cars I hadn't noticed. The Toyota wasn't going that fast, but within seconds it exited the highway, and disappeared from my view. I was amazed. I couldn't believe what the driver had done. What I witnessed was a new way of driving.

This modern style of driving is *late merging*. It is a simple set of maneuvers that allow you to move through lines of cars by spotting and filling in the gaps. Why wait? Late merging has the ability to transform lives—both behind the wheel and in our everyday life.

Since 2015, traffic on our highways has increased to highs of 36,210 VPH (vehicles per hour), despite more lanes being added.[1] Exit ramp lines continue to grow with more and more traffic gridlocked on our freeways.

Traffic engineers are doing everything possible to minimize traffic jams. HOV/HOT lanes have been installed on major thoroughfares, but these lanes aren't enough to speed up the traffic or prevent traffic jams. As residents move further away from their schools and work, the increased number of daily commutes continue to stall our roadways in numbers unimaginable to the original highway planners.

This book is organized in a way to help you reach your destinations quicker and enjoy life more—or as much as can be reasonably expected. In the following chapters, you'll learn ways to avoid these highway hazards and perfect the art of late merging on and off the road.

Best wishes for faster and more entertaining journeys,

Jenz

Jenz Johnson
San Diego, CA

1. Introduction

What is late merging?

Late merging is when a driver changes lanes near the front of the line politely and without disrupting traffic. It turns out to be the best way to drive these days on our crowded roadways.

Our cities have undergone major transformations in recent years, and late merging has created a new breed of driver, one who is unafraid to insert themselves into the challenges of highway traffic. The roadways of yesteryear are no longer able to accommodate the exponential increase in traffic, especially as people are forced to live further away from their jobs, schools, and families. New ways of driving are critical in navigating our freeways and city streets and living fuller lives.

If you fail to learn these new skills, you will literally be left behind.

In 2003 the Minnesota Department of Transportation confirmed that late merging improves throughput along highways by a factor of 17% and reduced queues by up to 33%.[2] In his ground-breaking book *Traffic*, author Tom Vanderbilt recommends that we should all practice the art of late merging.[3]

Late merging is also a mindset. With it, you'll be able to handle the long lines, traffic jams, and unruly drivers that are a constant reminder of the obstacles in daily life. Late merging requires concentration, courtesy, and intuition. It's all about finding openings.

Late merging can change your life

You may find something quite remarkable as you begin practicing this new way of driving. Late merging enables you to be more spontaneous. Behind the wheel of your own life, you're able to change directions or make decisions easily at a moment's notice.

This may be because, from a young age, we have been conditioned to believe that our lives should remain constant. We've been taught our careers should be carefully planned and followed. But in fact, such lives can be quite boring and do not take into consideration how everything around us is in a near-constant state of flux. We end up taking jobs below our capabilities, and settling for daily routines of bland meals, washing dishes, and watching the same reruns until we are too bored to stay awake. We become obsolete in our own lives.

Late merging revitalizes every facet of our being. It helps us overcome obstacles and avoid problems and delays. It simply makes us happier. It has become one of the most sought-after skills in our modern times.

To simply get in line and wait takes years off our lives. By saving 20 minutes in our daily commute each way, that's practically a full month each year we get back to spend with our friends and family doing the things we enjoy. This change can add years to your life. If you carried this into other areas, you could easily double it.

These skills change how you approach your daily routine, how you make decisions, and how you pursue your goals. (Refer to "Changing lanes can change your life" on page 50)

- **Moving up in the world.** Once you become adept at changing lanes in a variety of situations, you will be able to move up in the world using the same skill set.
- **Finding the right partner.** With more time on your hands and the ability to be with the people you enjoy the most, you can connect with potential future partners.
- **Expanding your horizons.** Late merging allows you to see the world with fresh eyes. You learn to navigate the edges of your current boundaries and find the points where you can simply step over.
- **Experiencing the excitement of something new.** With late merging, you are no longer bound by the same paths that everyone else adheres to. You're freed up to try new things.

Late merging is more than a driving maneuver: it is an invaluable life skill.

Why wait?

Why wait for reasons to move ahead?

This book covers the critical areas you need to master basic techniques of late merging. More importantly, it is the first step to a new you.

How to Read This Book

This book is meant to propel you into late merging in all aspects of your daily routines. You're encouraged to jump around based on your interests. If you're asleep at the wheel and unfamiliar with what to do in tight traffic, start with the initial chapters that cover the basics of merging. If you've mastered these skills on the road, then jump ahead to learn how these techniques can change your life.

- **Driving as an Art** explores the mindset behind late merging. Many view driving as the task of going the legal speed limit, staying between the lines, and turning on the correct streets. But it is much more. Your attitude plays an important part in your driving. It can help you to learn new techniques that are critical to late merging.
- **Merging Basics** details the basic maneuvers that can be used on the open road. It begins with the basic merge and then moves to more intricate tactics that require greater merging skills.
- **Hand Signals** have been all but forgotten by most drivers. Although left and right turns can be indicated by the left hand of the driver, they have been replaced by blinkers. What goes unused these days is the driver's right hand. Simple gestures have become a clear way to communicate with the drivers both in front and behind you. This chapter explains the different hand signals and their meaning.
- **Signs** offer a brief description of the traffic signs you encounter on the road and how they impact your driving. Knowing these signs and how to use them are critical in reaching your destination in a timely manner.
- **Driving Skills** provides a deep dive into switching lanes on both highways and city streets. Included are the keys to necessary maneuvers in and out of lanes, spotting gaps to facilitate late merges, being courteous and handling the types of drivers you encounter on the road.
- **Life Skills** is essential reading on how you can better adapt to the fast-changing world around us. There are key sections on how to be more spontaneous, how to make last-minute decisions, and how every aspect of your life can be more focused on moving ahead to ultimately live better.
- **Quick Guide** summarizes the lessons in this book and helps focus your life on the things that matter most.

The **Glossary** at the end provides a quick reference to terminology that can be helpful when discussing late merging.

2. Driving as an Art

Life is a race

Most of us drive the same way we were taught in Driver's Ed. We had little control over our lives at that time and we've kept our style of driving from that time. Perhaps you were closely supervised by your dear parents who wanted you to be the best version of yourself.

But with no disrespect to your loved ones, you must now be the person you want to be -- on and off the road. Your driving reflects your life and enhances your ability to see what's ahead. Meek accelerations and gentle turns will surely leave you behind. Every other car you'll notice is on the way to their destination and their drivers have little concern for you. Why? To put it bluntly, you're a stranger to them. How do they know who you really are?

Instead, you must realize that life is, in many ways, a zero-sum game. There is only a small percentage of people who can rise to the top to take home the prizes and glow in the awe of others.

Life is a race. And there is no better way to hone your competitive edge than on the road. It doesn't take a fancy car or a powerful engine to pull ahead of a line of cars on the freeway. Late merging is key to perfecting life skills that allow you to:

- See the openings ahead of you
- Get out from behind the slowpokes
- Be unafraid to drive faster in the slow lanes
- Avoid dummies that do dumb things
- Edge in between cars quickly when you see an opening

Freeways are our modern world in microcosm. Learning the ins and outs helps us to understand the world around us and how to navigate its complexities.

Finding the Flow

There is much talk these days about "getting into the Flow." This is just as true for driving as it is for the intricacies of daily life.

When you're *in the Flow*, everything seems to happen naturally: you are submerged in a world where openings appear without much effort. You let the speed of your car, the vision of cars ahead, and the gut feel of when there's an opening guide how you drive, turn, and connect.

For most roads, there is an intrinsic flow from the driver's perspective. That is, they can move at a certain rhythm based on the number of cars, the types of drivers and dummies, and the number of available lanes. From a highway engineering point of view, traffic flow is measured as the "number of cars passing some given point on the highway at a given time interval."[4] There are times when the freeway is so packed that no one moves, referred to as a Level of Service E—a road operating at capacity with irregular flow and virtually no usable gaps to maneuver in— which no one wants to experience.[5] Each highway can be evaluated on its capacity based on this level of service. The point here is to avoid Service E situations, since nothing you can do will move you anywhere up the queue.

Instead, move at a steady pace until you recognize an opening. Then focus on the cars around you so that you're *in the Flow*; be attentive and in tune with the drivers nearby. When there are lags (perhaps a car near you fails to keep up), it may be in your Flow to move into this gap as you edge forward.

Attaining the *Flow* requires the enjoyment of merging. Most drivers cannot see this, frustrated at the slowness of traffic. These drivers can turn into dummies around you, so it is important to avoid them. But for you, the *Flow* is where it's at.

What are speed limits for, exactly?

For those of you who have driven an autobahn in Germany, you know what it's like to whiz along without speed limits.

Invented in the first century AD by Emperor Claudius, the Via Portuensis ran from Rome to Ostia and was the first freeway as we understand it today. It was a multi-lane road with a center lane for pedestrians. It had neither speed limits nor any toga-wearing patrols in sandals to keep order. The first real autobahn ran from Milan to Varese in Italy and opened for traffic in 1924 with one lane for traffic in each direction.

The first German autobahn was opened in 1932 between Cologne and Bonn. Today there are multiple autobahns where speed limits are recommendations, not laws. The only law is the minimum speed limit of 60 km/h (or 37 mph). Vehicles unable to drive that fast (e.g., tractors, plows, and e-bikes) are not allowed on. Approximately 20% of autobahns have speed limits. On all others, motorists must adapt to the conditions. Drivers on the autobahn always stay in the right lane unless they are passing. A few cars have pushed their speeds on the autobahns to over 152 mph.

What makes the autobahn unique is the steadfastness of driver etiquette, specifically that slower vehicles drive in the right lane and all passing is done in lanes to their left. These are the rules. They don't apply to freeways in other countries, and in the U.S. this adherence to etiquette would be hard to find.

In the world of late merging, we are well withing the speed limits mainly because our freeways have slowed down between 20 to 40 mph. In traffic jams, they are stop-and-go's that never get effectively above 10 mph. Yet, if you find yourself with an open road in front of you and contemplate making up lost time due to earlier traffic, don't push the speed limit. Respect it. The challenge is finding the gaps that you can move into. The open road is a time to relax and enjoy some solitude with no cars near you to disrupt your reverie. It is a time to move freely in your lane.

If you find yourself in the thick of fast traffic, with cars in your lane going above the speed limit, you can always move to a slower lane.

Speed limits are there to remind you of the open road, of uncluttered travel that still exists on many rural roads. Most are reasonable speeds, so enjoy them. There's no real skill in flooring your gas pedal and roaring past other cars. Who cares if you know where your gas pedal is? Instead, roll down a window and enjoy the open road and the fact that you were able to reach the posted speed limit.

Being courteous while stepping forward

Since the days of elementary school when we lined up to go to class or to recess, we have been taught to get in line. Think back to your early school days. Did you ever join a friend near the front of the line? If your answer is no, then maybe you did not have many friends. Or you still hear the voice of your first-grade teacher reprimanding you for your brazen acts.

In fact, elementary school was where we made our first friends. And when you saw a friend near the front of the lunch line, someone you had lunch with most days, you could easily skip to the front and loudly say, "Thanks for saving me a place!"

It was well understood that having lunch with friends was at the top of everyone's list-- usually because most days this was the time that you could trade the carrots that your mom packed for something better.

The key was how you joined your friend. You needed acceptance from your other classmates, which you were so grateful for. You would turn to the person you were cutting in front of and ask, "Is this OK? We always have lunch together and today we're trying to squeeze in some tetherball." Hopefully you even said thank you.

Obviously, the reason for joining your friend was not as important as how grateful you were and how courteous you were. Any hesitation from the person and you could easily include, "Tomorrow you can cut in front of us. We really appreciate it today."

The same is true with merging. While most of us drive at a steady speed and stay in our lanes until we really need to leave the lane, others have appointments they are late for, or emergencies they need to attend to. We simply don't know why the person is in such a rush.

For late mergers, obviously, it's because of their way of life. Our mantra " लाइनोंसेबचें " (which loosely translated from Hindi means "don't sleep on mud floors") guides them in their drives each day and the challenges that they undertake on the road.

So, letting someone in front of you on the road just requires that the merge does not disrupt the *Flow* and that the driver is courteous. The driving part is easy. The courtesy part may take some practice since you must communicate it with hand gestures and blinking headlights occasionally.

The four steps to being courteous are:

1. Pull close to the gap and turn on your turn blinker.
2. With a hand gesture, wave your thanks.
3. Wait for their OK. This can be the blinking of their headlines or the driver giving you a thumbs up.
4. Merge into the lane, turn off your blinker and give a slightly bigger wave.

There is nothing fancy about showing your thanks. Some drivers tip their hats, but this is harder to understand. (Refer to Chapter 4 on page 19 for hand signals you can use on the road.)

3. Merging Basics

The Basic Merge

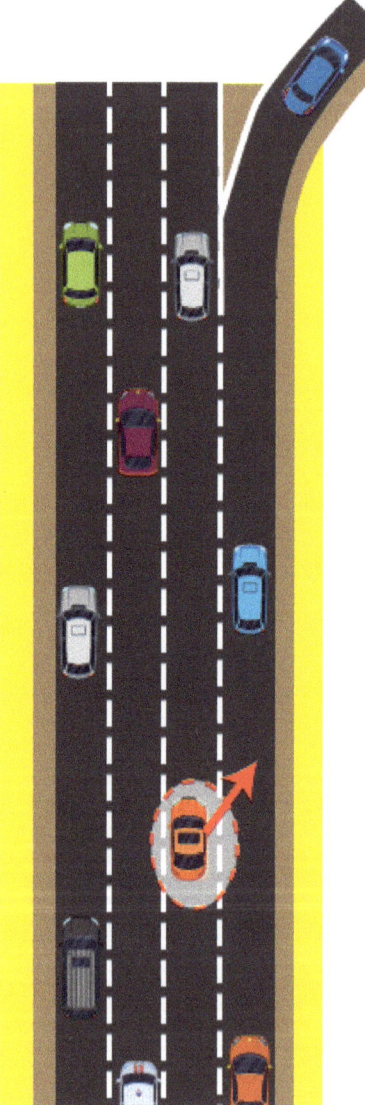

Merging is moving to an adjacent lane. It's best done when there is plenty of room between cars. A merge can get complicated when it is done too slowly: ideally the speed of your car should align with the cars in the next lane. Move next to the space in the next lane.

- Turn your right blinker on in plenty of time for the move.
- Glance in your rearview mirror to make sure that the car behind is still at a safe distance.
- Glance in your passenger side mirror to make sure another car has not snuck in.
- Move briskly into the lane and match your speed with the car in front.
- If there is a slowdown, apply your brake gradually to allow for the creation of distance in front without causing the car in back any difficulty.

The Basic Merge is a lane change we've all done before. There's plenty of room in the next lane and we're in no hurry.

The Early Merge

An Early Merge gets in line for the exit at the very back of the queue. Avoid this type of merging if at all possible. Regardless of the spacing elsewhere in the exit lane, the driver simply gets at the back, ignoring any openings.

There is no real technique to this type of merging, since it's a Basic Merge. Why would you want to do an Early Merge? The exit lane will slow down, so you will end up wasting time waiting for the cars to move. Doing this daily can trim years of your life by lulling you into waiting.

The Early Merge is a lane change we've all been taught. We catch the exit signs early on and can move over when the line is shorter. In rush hours, exit lines are usually quite long, and the wait can be quite numbing.

The Late Merge

The Late Merge is the way to go. It's done closer to the front of the line and requires searching for an opening (*aka* a gap) in the exit lane. Many times, motorists in the exit lane will make room in front. When a gap is spotted, the driver moves up and effortlessly merges into the lane without disruption.

- Wait for the opening to appear in the next lane. Be very patient and keep your focus.
- When you see the gap, turn on your right blinker and move up next to the spot.
- Before any next steps, make sure you check your mirrors.
- Be courteous, maybe point with your free hand and wait for permission to continue.
- Move calmly into the lane.
- When you are fully in the lane, give a courteous hand wave as your thanks.

There is a good deal of technique involved in a Late Merge, and situations can occur that drivers should be aware of. But the result is you have not spent too much time waiting in long lines during rush hour. Although the spaces near the front seems harder to reach and maneuver into, it will become easier the more you practice on your daily commutes.

The Reverse Late Merge

The Reverse Late Merge uses the exit lane to bypass vehicles to the left. It's counterintuitive. It happens when there are exit lanes with very few cars. Instead of trying to find gaps, the driver gets into the exit lane and uses it to pass other cars. Typically, the driver can find a gap to move back onto the main lane. When the opening is just before the exit lane splits off the highway, it is the epitome of a Reverse Late Merge.

The same steps are used:

- Stay in the exit lane and move slowly, keeping an eye on the lane to your left.
- Wait for an opening.
- When you spot the gap, turn on your left blinker.
- Check your mirrors.
- Be courteous.
- Move into the lane with a hand wave.

Many times, exit lanes move at a brisk pace with fewer cars. But as with a normal Late Merge, the Reverse Late Merge requires keeping an eye on gaps to change lanes, as well as encouraging drivers in the exit lane to move to the main highway whenever possible. Blinking your headlights can encourage this.

The Tight Merge

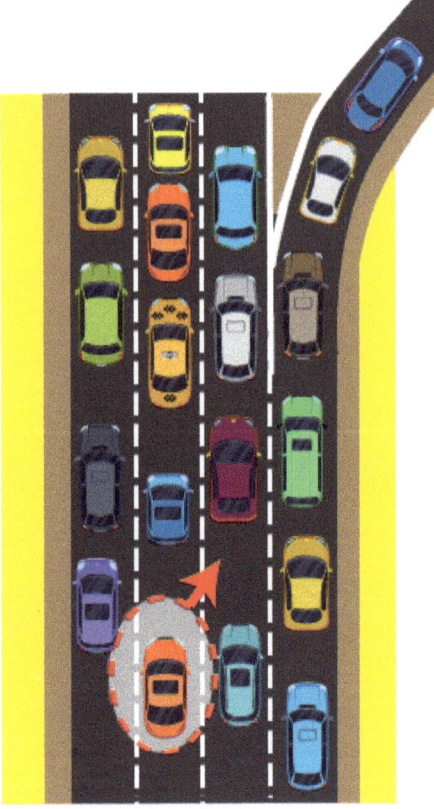

In making our way across the lanes, whether they are early or late merges or simply crossovers, the driver will find many situations where the gaps are not as big as they would like it. These situations require *tight merges*.

These merges use a simple technique of focusing on the driver to your right. It is this driver who can make a difference. Keep even with the driver as the traffic slows to stop and go. At the next spurt of flow, this car may lag just enough to let you in. Of course, it may be a lapse in concentration that created this space but interpret it as the driver inviting you to join them in their lane.

- Wait for the gap to lengthen.
- Turn on your right blinker.
- Check your mirrors.
- Be courteous.
- Move into the lane with a hand wave.

For zigzagging this can happen multiple times as you move forward. Be friendly and attentive to the spaces that momentarily open.

The Pre-Merge

To prepare for a Late Merge, the driver needs to spot the space that they are aiming at, then pull up to the car right behind the space.   Accelerating just a tad, the driver pulls up and puts on their right blinker, signaling that they intend to merge ahead of the car.

At this point, the driver of the other car can close the space off, but usually if the merger identifies the gap in the queue, they are entitled to merge. This maneuver is the Pre-Merge.

Hand signals (covered in Chapter 4) are essential for these maneuvers, as well as a friendly smile as you pass by.

The Crossover

When drivers are in fast-moving or HOV lanes and must make an upcoming exit, they must be skilled at *crossovers*. As the name suggests, it is performing late merges across multiple lanes aiming at a final merge into the exit lane. The driver has their eye on a gap in the exit lane and the time needed to reach it.

The key is recognizing just how much time will be needed to reach the final gap in the exit lane. For HOV lanes where drivers are required to have multiple occupants or drive a qualified EV, they must exit over the dashed white lines of their lane. Crossing over solid white or yellow lines can result in a ticket.

Beginners should allow plenty of time for their crossovers. But skilled late mergers can execute crossovers with little advanced warning.

Courtesy remains critical since you are asking other drivers to allow you in. There may be an advantage to this advanced maneuver since other motorists recognize your need to move to the exit. It also frees up your space in the fast lane, which is usually welcomed.

4. Hand Signals

Basic Hand Signals

Hand signals are the best way to communicate with other drivers. With one hand on the steering wheel, express yourself with your right hand. To do them, you must (1) have a good hold of your steering wheel, (2) keep your focus on the road and traffic, and (3) resist lingering in your rearview mirror to see if the driver behind you sees your gesture.

From the back, hand signals are easy to recognize when merging or passing. Use your blinkers for turns and to signal moving into the next lane.

You can use the following hand signals:

The Wave

The most common gesture is the wave. It is a courteous way to thank the driver behind you as you move into the lane. Continue to wave as you get into the flow of your new lane.

Thumbs Up

The thumbs-up hand signal indicates success. It expresses the results of your maneuver and can communicate with the driver that assisted you. For example, the driver slowed down to let you in. When you arrive in the lane, a thumbs up means that your lane change worked, and they were key to your success.

Palm Up

An open palm up signal is used to ask the basic question *hey what's up?* Sometimes when a driver performs an odd maneuver in front of you, you can follow it with an open palm as if to say, *what was that?* Or if you do an unusual maneuver that you can't explain, an open palm confirms that you didn't know what you just did.

The Point

When you need to draw attention to some activity or sign along the road, you can point to it with your free hand. The Point is usually for the benefit of the driver behind you or in the lane next to you. Sometimes there is a sign that the driver did not see. Other times it can indicate that you are planning to move into the next lane ahead of the driver. When combined with your blinker, it is very effective in getting the driver's attention.

Left Turn

When you extend your hand out your window for a left-hand turn, it is usually accompanied by your left-turn blinker. Do this to emphasize that you really want to move into this lane. You'll see it used as on-ramps merge into the highways. When it is close and you see a small gap, this hand signal definitely helps.

The Finger (Don't Do It).

Regardless of your experience on the road, it makes no sense to communicate your anger to another driver. Even if they are dummies or do stupid maneuvers that can result in accidents, giving the other driver the finger is uncalled for. Instead, try a wave. It communicates the fact that you avoided their stupidity in a courteous way.

Ear Poke

Many times, you may see mergers using the ear poke gesture. This is often misinterpreted as "I could just kill myself" instead of what is most likely an ear itch, so should not be used.

Of all the hand signals, it is recommended that you practice the Wave. It is useful in many situations and can communicate your thanks to other drivers assisting you. For left merges, many drivers will point with their left hand out the window to reinforce their intention of moving over. In some situations, that may make sense, especially if the driver behind you is asleep at the wheel or doesn't seem to notice the pre-merge moves.

5. Signs

Although most drivers are familiar with speed limits and most highway signs, there are several signs that should be emphasized. Among them are the following:

Exit Ahead

As you drive to your destination, you should be on the lookout for the exit you need to take. One of the first indications is the Exit Ahead sign. This will give you plenty of time to late merge in the exit lane, so long as you are next to it. If not, begin crossing over and wait for your opportunity to move close to the front in the exit lane from an adjacent lane.

Next Exit

You should be in your final position to late merge when you see the Next Exit sign. This indicates that the exit lane will separate from the highway. Many late mergers wait until they see this sign to begin their merge, but you can certainly start before you see the sign.

Highway Splits

The most exciting signs to see along the freeway are the ones that announce splits. These occur when one side continues in the same direction, while another splits off. Most drivers make their choices earlier. But late mergers usually wait until the last quarter mile to arrange to move over. This allows plenty of time and helps perfect their traffic skills.

Lane Ends

If you are in the far-right lane and you encounter this sign, it is a good time to check for gaps to your left and the perfect time to practice your late merging. So often late merging happens to your right: when you need to merge to the left, wait until the last moment, turn your left blinker on, give a wave, then merge over.

Divided Highway Ahead

Most drivers are used to divided highways, but when you are on a country road or side streets, be aware of signs that inform you of a divided highway up ahead. When this sign appears, it is usually a good indication that you'll have a passing lane to the left. It is the right time to get into the fast lane and pull ahead. Avoid the median at all costs.

25

Divided Highway Ends

As your highway slows into a city street, the lanes will pull together, preventing any passing into oncoming traffic. When this sign appears, make your final merge before getting in line. If the city street has at least two lanes in each direction, pull into the fast lane and begin looking ahead for zigzag opportunities. Remember courtesy is very important. You can also wave to oncoming cars as a friendly greeting.

Cattle Ahead

Nothing can be more surprising than to learn that cattle are allowed on the road. You may be traveling at the speed limit when you see this sign. It's a good time to slow down and wave to the cowboys and their herd.

Snowmobiles Ahead

It can be equally surprising to find out there may be snowmobiles on the road ahead. Although this happens less in the summer and spring, it is still a good idea to keep an eye out ahead. If you plan to pass or merge, you may need to adjust your side mirror down to catch these smaller vehicles.

Horseback Riding Allowed

More and more, our roads are open to a variety of vehicles. In rural areas, you may find some locals travel on horseback. This is a pleasurable way to travel, even if it is just for a leisurely weekend jaunt. If you are driving, try to avoid any deposits of poop on the road. Refrain from honking or any other loud activity that might frighten the horse or its rider.

6. Driving Skills

Don't be a dummy

Dummies are drivers that do stupid things. The simple fact is that we can all be dummies at one time or another. All it takes is a distraction. These can be as dumb as checking your hair or playlist or adjusting your mirrors while you're driving. Take your eyes and attention off the road and you have disconnected. Anything goes at this point. You may slip into becoming a dummy.

You can tell a dummy based on a few oddball activities you see them perform on the highway, including:

- **Laggy Lags.** These are lags in their lane that last too long. There's no requirement to keep too lengthy a distance from the car in front. But when this does not happen at random times, the driver is a dummy. You should be weary.
- **Wobbly Side-to-Sides.** If the driver is too close to one side of their lane, i.e., wobbling, then they are most likely a dummy. Keep your distance.
- **Lane Blocking.** If the driver is at a standstill and blocking an exit lane, they are truly a dummy. Simply stopping in this way is asking for trouble.
- **Spurts.** If the driver speeds up then slows down without any reason, aka spurting, they are acting like dummies. So, treat them as such.

We must all drive predictably. We cannot be distracted even for moments during sing-along's when we finally remember the lyrics. Concentration and courtesy should rule the day.

If you have occupants that are disruptive, then you must settle them down without taking your eyes off the road or losing your focus.

We all have the capacity to be dummies. It is important to recognize them on the road and avoid getting close to them at all costs.

Doing the right thing

You may find yourself in a discussion of whether late merging is morally the *right* thing to do. That is, does it fly in the face of everything we've been taught is proper? To be clear, late merging makes the lives of our fellow travelers quicker and happier. But is it the right thing to do from an ethical perspective? On this, you'll be on solid ground.

Late merging abides by the Golden Rule: "Do unto others as you would have them do unto you." This tenet appears in some form in almost every major religious tradition in the world and is widely viewed as one of the common denominators connecting most—if not all—faith communities. Confucius stated it as a negative: "What you do not wish for yourself, do not do to others," which is functionally identical to Hillel's "What is hateful to you, do not do to your fellow." Those drivers who invite mergers in are signaling that it is perfectly fine and that they may do the same one day. Agnostics also embrace the concept, as they have nothing morally to lose.

Ralph Cudworth (1617-88) and his philosophy of *intuitionism* asserted that we have the ability to determine right and wrong through our own rational intuition. We intuitively know that it is morally correct to allow a car to move in front of us if their need to do so is evident. Oliver Wendell Holmes Jr. (1841-1935) and The Metaphysical Club understood the world around us through our experiences and from it, our ethical norms. [6] This is the moral philosophy of *pragmatism*. Communities are drawn together by their pragmatic experiences and the positive impact on their lives. In this way, late merging encourages others to practice ways to make their commutes faster and more exciting for the good of the driving community.

Most highway travelers embrace late merging as a technique that emboldens a new pragmatic standard on our roadways. From a variety of perspectives, it is the right thing to do.

Disciplined Driving Demeanor (DDD)

The key to late merging and overall traffic safety is being able to maintain a *disciplined driving demeanor* (DDD). This is a mindset that continually focuses on the road and your surroundings. You should concentrate on the lane that you are planning to late merge into, while keeping an eye on other vehicles in other lanes. DDD requires that you constantly check your mirrors and be on the lookout for any dummies close by or drivers that may lurch unexpectedly into adjoining lanes.

The key to safe driving is to always be on the lookout. Keeping your focus on what's around you will keep you and your passengers safe. It is active meditation that you must train yourself to practice every time you pull out of your driveway and head out to the open road.

Getting in and out of HOV/HOT lanes

On many freeways these days, the left-most lane is reserved for electronic vehicles (EVs) and high occupancy vehicles (HOV) with two or more occupants. In some cases, it is a high-occupancy toll (HOT) lane where drivers can use the lane if they pay a toll.

Regardless of the type of vehicle or occupancy, if you are qualified to drive in this lane, you can. (The fines are steep if you're not, so be careful.) The problem arises when you are getting in and out of the lane, which can only happen at dashed lines. Crossing over solid or double white or yellow lines is not allowed. If you are stuck behind a slowpoke, or can't exit the HOV lane in time for your exit, is it worth it?

The key is the distance to your next exit. If it is a fairly large number of miles, then using the HOV lane when you qualify makes sense. Otherwise, it only takes one slowpoke to hold up the entire entourage. You're much better off finding the gaps along the way and zigzagging your way to faster traffic. Although HOV lanes can make the commute faster at times, it suffers from the same drawbacks of normal rush hours: too many cars in lanes built for a lower volume.

Enjoying the landscape and conversations

Can you enjoy your surroundings and conversation while driving? This is a common question that is asked, since these can be distractions that lure you into a dummy state. That is, you are not focusing on your driving and instead are trying to make a point.

Now the point may be well taken and the passenger whose comment needs pushback can use the opportunity to their advantage. This is also the case when you are traveling through captivating mountains, and your passenger wants you to share the experience.

What can you do?

Unfortunately, your attention must be fully on the road if there is traffic around you. Your ability to

find and move into gaps will be needlessly hindered by distracting conversations and gorgeous vistas. Quick glances are OK for the scenery and an occasional "that's dumb" response can keep your passenger's argument sated.

When traffic subsides and there is an easy-to-maintain flow, you can relax and engage more. But be forewarned that this can change at a moment's notice, and you must be prepared to continue a disciplined driving demeanor (DDD). This state of driving involves concentrating on the road in front of you, the drivers close by and potential merges coming up. It requires that you constantly check your mirrors and be focused on any potential dummies that are straggling behind. (Refer to page 32 for more information.)

In short, enjoying conversations and landscape should be left to your passengers. You can pitch in on occasion, but do not make a habit of these endeavors.

Driving safely

It is impossible to know what drivers around us are doing or thinking. They could be texting on their phones or in the midst of a conference call. Their attention may be diverted from everything that really matters -- like their own safety and the safety of those around them. At any moment these drivers can slip into *stupid driving*. This is a prelude to becoming full-fledged *dummies*. They may merge into your lane when there's no room, or weave around in their own lanes as they adjust their audio channel or fumble for their sunglasses.

At any moment, you and your passengers could be at the mercy of these dummies. They may be in the lanes next to you, or up ahead. Suddenly there is a stream of brake lights rippling toward you. You must simply be prepared for the unexpected.

The skills learned in late merging become critical in your ability to avoid accidents and respond to dummies. In particular,

- **Keep your focus on the road**. It goes without saying that your attention should not be diverted by conversations around you or by distractions within your vehicle.
- **Be prepared to merge**. Although you will become proficient at finding gaps in lines of cars, these same skills can be used to avoid swerving by stupid drivers into your own lane. These techniques can also help you to avoid unexpected objects in the road.
- **Check your mirrors frequently.** Incidents can also happen behind you when a driver does not slow down quickly enough. So, keep an eye on your rearview mirror and side mirrors.

These and other skills are described in more detail in the sections ahead. You'll be able to respond in a way that does not disrupt those around you. It is the safest way to drive.

Driving in fast lanes

We have a misconception that the fast lanes to the far left on a multi-lane freeway are the ones that go the fastest. After all, that is their intent.

On German autobahns, this is certainly the case. But in the U.S. the fast lanes may be the slowest depending on the intelligence of the drivers. This is because everyone wants to go faster. Who can blame them? But driving in the fast lanes only works if there is a constant flow and the cars are moving faster than the other lanes.

If you are trying to exit, fast lanes can challenge you with crossovers. These are maneuvers that require that you cross over multiple lanes to get to your desired exit. (Refer to The Crossover on page 18 to learn the basic steps involved.)

If cars in the fast lane are moving at a faster speed than those to their right, it makes good sense to stay in the fast lane. As these vehicles slow down, keep an eye on the other lanes up ahead. You may find that these lanes are not moving any faster. If so, just stay put. Use fast lanes as you would any other lane. They are easy to zigzag in and out of, and the drivers can be just as accommodating.

Zigzagging avoids slowdowns

As traffic moves in dribs and drabs, it is advisable to begin zigzagging to find a faster path through the lanes. This entails moving side to side to pass slower cars. The technique is still finding gaps, but there is less emphasis on late merging. Instead use tight merging techniques.

Zigzagging can move both left and right depending on the flow. Do not move in or out of HOV/HOT lanes unless there are dashed lines that allow it. You may find multiple cars practicing zigzagging on your stretch of the road. This can make your maneuvering even more enjoyable since it turns it into a race of sorts.

You may also find the cars that stick to their lanes and don't zigzag wind up winning this race. This usually indicates that your technique needs some polishing. Don't abandon zigzagging when you find yourself behind the driver that sticks to their lane. Yours has been an enjoyable adventure with the challenge of finding the faster lanes and moving into them when the appropriate gap opens.

When to honk at slowpokes

When you are at a traffic light and the lead car doesn't move on when the light changes to green, there is usually an orchestra of honks that spurs them into action. This can be the driver simply catching up on their text messages at a safe time or scrolling through their podcasts. Whatever the reason, the litany of honks shakes them awake and they move across the intersection. This is also the case for other cars in line at a traffic light.

These types of slowpokes need polite honks to get them going. A polite honk is a softer toot which serves as a reminder that the light has changed.

On a busy freeway, polite honking is discouraged because it affects the demeanor of the drivers already caught in stop-and-go jams. Instead, try blinking your headlines. Usually, you are close enough to catch the other driver's attention. They will usually respond quickly and move forward.

Alternatively, when you find a slowpoke ahead, they may in fact be helping you by encouraging you to begin zigzagging. This type of reaction to slowpokes is a welcome change since it adds a certain excitement to your drive. In this way slowpokes can be helpful. They provide more gaps on the road and ways for you to move ahead.

Also keep in mind that we all are slowpokes at one time or another. The most common cause of this is losing our focus and not keeping up with the cars in front of us.

When you are at traffic lights or four-way stops and the car in front of you is not moving, a polite honk can work. On the freeway with stop-and-go traffic, blink your headlights and consider some zigzagging to spice up your drive.

Don't let big trucks bully you

Trucks can have some of the biggest gaps in front of them. This is because they have heavier loads and can't accelerate like a normal vehicle. In this way they become our friends on the freeway. They will let you in when there is a gap.

Many times, though, if you are zigzagging you may find trucks moving closely together with little room for you to merge. Don't push it. Driving between two large trucks with a lot of momentum from their freight may not be the most relaxing. It may feel like you're in a waffle maker. You may continually hear the hiss of their brakes and be glued to your rearview mirror. In these situations, it is best to move in front of the lead truck.

Don't let them bully you because of their size. If you need to late merge into an exit lane and there is a truck with a nice gap in front, turn on your turn blinker and wait for them to reply. If there is no reply but you have good clearance, begin your merge.

In most cases truck drivers are some of the more professional drivers on freeways. They will blink their headlights to let you in and their taillights when you return the favor. Imagine spending your days on the road and having to make progress every day through traffic slowdowns. Truck drivers have the patience, skills, and camaraderie to make your freeway experience a positive one.

Don't tap your brakes to make a point

From time to time, you may find the car behind you on the freeway is tailing you too closely. That is, the space between your car and theirs is too tight.

They may have a good reason for this:

- They want to prevent any merging in front of them.
- They may be sending you a signal to speed up.
- They may feel the distance is quite natural for the speed the traffic is at.

Whatever their response, resist tapping your brake to send your message: back *up dummy!* This creates a ripple effect. When you tap your brake, the car behind panics and can brake harder than they need to. Then the car behind them does the same. This can lead to rear-enders and bumper accidents.

Instead, gradually slow down so that the car decides to either pass you or moves back a safe distance. A quick wave communicates that you are doing so in a friendly manner. If they blink their headlights, simply wave back.

The way you communicate and the friendliness you exhibit should help resolve the matter. If not, merge into another lane to give the car the ability to pass. In fact, in any situation, if the cars behind you are moving at a quicker clip than you, just move over to let them by.

Waving when irritated cars pass by

The goal of freeway driving is not to be popular. And in situations of late merging, you may find other drivers become irritated at your proximity. Keep in mind that you are not performing your maneuvers with or for the other driver. They just happen to be in line. And you are not judgmental

that they are exhibiting slowpoke or dummy behavior: that is their choice from simply losing their driving focus.

When you run into a driver who is visibly upset and seems to be motioning at you with a free hand, do not engage them in car-to-car conversations. As they pass by in an irritable state, do not add to their sense of being insulted. Your gliding into a spot in front of them was no doubt graceful. Instead, use the moment to establish your continued courtesy and friendliness, regardless of the other driver's agitation.

- To acknowledge their frenzied state, give them a friendly wave. The message you are sending is that you appreciate their feedback. Which you do.
- If they are trying to talk with you, even with their window closed, acknowledge whatever point they are making with a gentle nod, as if to say *yes, I get it*.
- If they are trying to merge in front of you, even with some lurches or lags, invite them in to join your lane. Scooch back to show your willingness to foster a renewed interest in merging.

In short, be pleasant with an irritated driver. They may have had a long day that did not go well. Maybe they spent their time thinking about the ups and downs at work, instead of focusing on initiating some zigzagging or crossovers on the way home.

Keep an eye on blind spots

No matter how well you adjust your side mirrors, you will still be stuck with blind spots. These become important as you navigate toward a merging opportunity. As focused as you are on the car in front of you and those in the lane next to you, you may overlook those drivers who have snuck into one of your blind spots.

Many times, dummies don't realize where they are. They may stay in these spots thinking that they are able to take advantage of drafting next to your vehicle. The only protection you have is to move up, so they are clearly in your side mirror, or to fall back so you are side by side. In this way you can keep track of them.

It is also important that you avoid blind spots of the cars next to you. On the open road, this means moving ahead of them in the next lane. A casual hand wave is always helpful.

In many modern vehicles, your side mirror will blink a warning if it detects cars in blind spots next to you. These turn into beeps if you have your right blinker on. For older vehicles a simple glance over your shoulder before you begin to merge can ensure that there are no vehicles lingering in these areas.

Pay attention to these areas on both sides of the car since they can be the cause of unwanted encroachments.

Adjusting your mirrors *en route*

As a rule of thumb, adjust your mirrors before you pull out onto a public road. If you are entering your destination into Google Maps or traffic app, use the time to double-check your mirrors. After you stop for coffee or tea, check your mirrors again before continuing your drive.

At some point though, you may notice that your mirrors are out of whack while you are driving. Adjusting them takes the same level of concentration as merging. Keep in mind that there will be cars on either side of you trying to pass, or cars behind you suddenly changing course.

This means that your adjustment must happen in clear steps while maintaining your concentration on the road.

- **Pause any zigzagging or merging.** Maybe you discovered your misaligned mirrors during a maneuver. If so, find a stable lane with plenty of space.   You can pick up from where you left off after you've corrected your mirrors.
- **Fix your rearview mirror.** This mirror can frame a good deal of activity both behind and to the side of you. So, it makes sense to adjust this with your free right hand. Do not look at yourself in the mirror, since you may find some personal points of interest that throw you off.
- **Do not roll down any windows.** If your side mirrors can only be adjusted manually by rolling down your windows, do not attempt this while in motion. Wait for the next stop when you are at a standstill.
- **Adjust your side mirrors.** Your side mirrors are extremely important as they can catch cars moving into your blind spot before it occurs. The key to their position is aligning the side of your car with the nearest edge of the side mirror.

This way, as cars behind you make moves to pass or those in either lane move forward, you will be able to spot them and incorporate them into any moves you undertake.

One-handed driving tips

Throughout your drive, you will occasionally need a free hand for gestures. They can be as simple as a wave, but without some way to communicate from your driver's seat, you will not be able to encourage the type of friendly driving that will make a difference on the road.

One-handed driving has gotten a bad rap, mainly because people attempt turns or merging with one hand. This is a no-no. Instead, follow these guidelines:

- Grasp the steering wheel at the top (12:00). Before taking your right hand off, take your left elbow off the arm rest of the driver's side door. Then move it to the top of the steering wheel. Keep your arm straight. Grasp the steering wheel firmly. You should be able to steer easily.
- Keep your focus as you lift your right hand. This means being aware of traffic around you as you lift one hand off the steering wheel.
- Always keep your eyes on the road. Even though you may be attending to other matters in your car or gesturing, keep your eyes on the road.

Place your right hand back when you are finished with your gesture or taking a much-needed sip of coffee.

Checking yourself in the rearview mirror

Often, drivers are on their way to an engagement or presentation and do not check whether their hair or makeup are in place. So, you'll see these drivers pull close to their rearview mirror or even tilt their mirrors toward themselves. If their car is moving, this is ill-advised. It is an indication that

their focus is intentionally lapsed and the awareness of cars around them is handicapped.

If you're behind them, flashing your headlights may have little effect: they're looking at themselves. Honking is not recommended either since it should be used only in dire circumstances to prevent collisions.

Instead, it is time to change lanes and pull ahead. Look to the lane next to you to see if there is a gap. If so, begin the process of changing lanes. It is difficult to admonish drivers who do things wrong in front of you, especially if they cannot see you. Instead, simply time to move on.

If they return their mirror to its correct position, and glance back, you might give them a Palm Up hand sign (with a shrug) to indicate a question: *What was that*? Follow it with a wave to indicate no hard feelings.

Our job on the freeway is to be agile, to move easily across lanes and find the gaps that we can use to swiftly move up the lanes. We are not traffic instructors or the highway patrol. When someone drives in an usual way or you see them taking their focus away from driving, stay neutral but point out your disbelief that they did what they did.

Letting others in is playing it forward

Late merging is a two-way street (so to speak). When you see a driver next to you and there is a small opening in front of you, invite them in by slowing down a bit. This is *playing it forward*. The more you allow cars to late merge as the exits approach, the more you'll find generous drivers doing the same for you.

The act of allowing cars to merge into your lane helps you to understand other drivers and the fact that not everyone on the road is driving for the same reasons. Some are trying to get home to their families as quickly as possible, while others are casually driving to the store or to nowhere in particular. The impetus to merge may not be present in the minds of many drivers. Others may need to merge for whatever reason, even if it is to perfect their late merging skills.

Letting these drivers in also gives you a chance to observe their technique. You may pick up a hand signal that you like or see how they adjust their speed when their merge begins.

Make eye contact or at least give them a friendly wave in response to theirs. These types of courtesies will help your Merging Karma (on the next page).

When you see an excellent merge and acknowledge it, you will be building your own skills through your observations.

Merging Karma

Many drivers who attempt late merging may find that there are few openings near the exits for them to move into. This happens and should not deter a driver from continuing their efforts. But many times, it is also a reflection of their Merging Karma.

Merging Karma is basically your karma on the road. Gaps will magically open when your karma is good. That is, when you have allowed other cars to late merge into your lane just before your exit, you will be earning the equivalent of karma points. You let cars in, not because it builds your Merging Karma, but because it was a friendly thing to do. Just because you found a great gap to move into does not mean that you don't allow others to have the same joy you feel in your accomplishment.

Your Merging Karma can also be affected by any ill feelings you have for drivers doing the wrong things. You can shake your head when a driver causes near misses or is discourteous to others. But you can't vent over the actions, using inappropriate hand signals to show your displeasure. We are all human. We make mistakes. We build our Merging Karma by showing others how it can be done and by letting other mergers in.

Winning important discussions in the car

Driving with friends, family and coworkers may be the perfect opportunity to discuss important issues. When traffic is bumper to bumper and everyone is together, there's less opportunity for chitchat to be interrupted. The problem comes when you are trying to merge or find the new gaps in front of you. What are you supposed to do? A lapse in focus is not good in heavy traffic, but then again, making a winning point may not come your way again.

The simple answer is to pause the conversation. If it is a merge you are undertaking, begin with *here's my point*... but then hold that thought until you're finished merging. Maybe interject with *just a sec, I'm almost done here*. Should anyone try to interrupt, just caution them it's not a good time for them to speak.

When you have completed your merge, slow to the correct speed and continue with *like I was saying, my point is*... and continue with your argument. Make your point, then as a driver, suggest they move the discussion until later when it's safer. Who can object? By that time, who knows, maybe the same friends or coworkers are not together, or they forget about it altogether. In either case, you've won that round of discussion, plus you've made a successful merge while your passengers remained quiet.

Talking while driving in uncluttered traffic with a lot of space between cars is usually fine. As the traffic turns into a tighter squeeze, take control of the conversations that you want to be a part of, and guide them as you attempt your merge and keep an eye on cars in front of you.

Changing lanes before there's space

There are times when you know you're going to be late. Maybe you're running late for work (which your coworkers will forgive, but probably not your supervisor). Or maybe you have a meet-up or date waiting for you at a coffee shop or restaurant. In these cases, the pressure is on. Late merging can be a real lifesaver.

But these situations can put undue pressure on you to make the merge. You may find yourself moving in a lane where there is little space.

What can be done when you find yourself up against a brick wall? Do you try to squeeze in? Do you honk for attention? Do you give up?

All of these options are running through your head as you try to figure out what to do. You're already late: taking an alternative route will only add more time and frustration. Giving up seems like pure defeat. And frankly, it is. Your situation may simply be due to your inability to find the gaps, or you may have a driver in the exit lane who is not inviting you in.

Before you give up entirely, check for gaps. Use your rearview mirror to see if you mistakenly passed up a better spot to merge earlier in the exit lane. It happens. If it is close and you can slow down to line up with this gap, you may be in luck. However, if you wreak havoc on the exit lane, then be courteous and just move on. There is little that you can do but forego the late merge. It's a hard lesson, but endangering drivers around you as you try to creep in only makes you the creep.

By learning the maneuvers and suggestions in this book, you will find that these situations become very rare, and that you'll almost always be able to late merge.

For now, be courteous and move on.

7. Life Skills

Changing lanes can change your life

Perfecting one's skills on freeways can improve your commute times, brighten up your drive with challenges, and spread courteous behavior between drivers. Driving on freeways does not need to be boring or stressful.

In fact, with the proper skills and outlook, you can look forward to your morning and evening commutes with the same expectation you'd have of being with friends. On the road, you find and fill the gaps while avoiding lines.

Yet what becomes more apparent is that these skills carry over to your daily life as well.

Of course, there are those that consider waiting in line to be a valuable pastime. One can contemplate the universe[7] and begin to treasure the small details of life. Others have much better things to do than wait. What we don't realize is that late merging can focus a person on the present and open a world filled with gaps and opportunities to navigate. The ability to see the world in this light and, most importantly, to navigate its obstacles and openings, can serve to expand one's experience. It can be useful in a variety of other settings:

- **Moving up in the world.** If moving over seems possible and in fact well within your framework to conquer, then moving up in your class or workplace presents the same situation. There are those in the queue for promotions, leading with their work and reputation, while others flail about trying to get home at a reasonable hour. (For remote workers, it means being able to look up from your desk to spend mealtime with your family.) But late merging can change your position in the promotion queue with subtle steps to the front that catch the attention of middle managers and higher-ups.

- **Finding the right partner.** When you are free to pursue those interests that have intrigued you for so long and attend the parties and dinners you've been wanting to experience, you become a more interesting person. You'll engage in subjects that interest you in conversation without just waiting for your turn to speak. You are courteous but enthusiastic. Many people talk about weather or get themselves enmeshed in politics. However, when you see the important things in your life and pursue them without hesitation, your passion will attract others with the same inclinations. Within shorter periods of time, you begin to find people you are attracted to and do not wait to engage them.

- **Expanding your horizons.** When you jump into adventures and activities because they excite you, you begin to see the world with fresh eyes. You don't need all the skill sets to start out. And you can learn on the fly as you navigate the edges of your current boundaries.

- **Experiencing the excitement of something new.** You are no longer bound by the same paths that everyone else adheres to. You respect their choices, but their choices aren't yours. Give yourself permission to try new things, to step into new lines and move to the front with curiosity, enthusiasm, and generosity. Those around you will be touched by your open-eyed embrace of a new activity. They will learn from your mistakes (if you make any) and will also learn not to take themselves too seriously.

As you simply avoid lines and wait for what everyone else waits for, you will discover your passions. There is a lot more doing and less analysis as you perfect this life skill of late merging.

Living longer by avoiding lines

When we see lines, our first inclination is to get into the shortest one. We've been told since we were toddlers to do just that. If we are in a grocery store near dinner time when the crowds clog the aisles and lines are everywhere, how are we going to find the shortest path? It's not only driving to the store that has taken time, but now we are in the store and see the same motion of shoppers trying to get in the line the fastest.

The key is to avoid lines altogether. Once you accept that you'll need to stand in line, you are essentially pausing your life. That's not living. In many instances, of course, you have no choice. The store is thinly staffed; the shoppers are in a hurry; there are items missing and the shopping carts no longer steer correctly. Once in line shoppers usually organize themselves at the last moment, trying to find coupons, or struggling with their credit cards or counting out the pennies for the exact amount in cash.

There are many in the academic community and elsewhere that emphasize that this kind of waiting is beneficial to everyone around them.[8] Waiting in line makes us aware of how fleeting our lives are, and that we are only on this earth for a relatively short period of time. This realization should be grasped and meditated on as we wait. It helps us to realize the meaninglessness of life itself[9] which to some may be a good thing.

But the reality is that we aren't going to be meditating in this fashion nor contemplating the meaninglessness of life as we try to figure out why our line has stalled. These types of reflections belong on a yoga mat with gentle music in the background, and a place to stretch and rest.

Instead, the key to prolonging our lives is not to wait in line. Now this may seem impossible during a shopping rush hour. Going to a store that is packed flies in the face of the basic principle of avoiding lines.

The solution is shopping during off-hours. Instead of walking into your favorite store around dinner time, shop midafternoon, or even during dinner hours when suddenly cashiers are freed up and the lines shorten or dry up entirely.

In other words, timing is everything.

Instead of taking your lunch hour at a normal time, move it into late morning or midafternoon. Use this time to shop at nearby stores. If it is for groceries, keep the items in your trunk. If they require refrigeration, check into using your company's fridge. You may even find that an ice chest in your car works just fine for these late afternoon shopping times.

If you still find yourself occasionally in crowds at stores, keep an eye on the checkout lines. You will find that even in heavy shopper traffic, many lines simply open up. Make a quick dash to these cashiers.

There are a number of remedies for avoiding lines in our daily lives. It takes a bit of creativity to figure out the best times. It is much like late merging on the road since you are keeping an eye on the best times to avoid lines.

It's never too late

For late merging, it's never too late.

When you see your exit approach and the cars do not seem to be letting you in, don't worry. It's almost never too late to make the move. The same perspective applies to our daily lives. When we think about the future and how we want it to be different, we many times rush our decisions, thinking we'll run out of time if we don't act quickly. For example, if you've been contemplating changing jobs and have missed a few openings at other companies, don't give up.

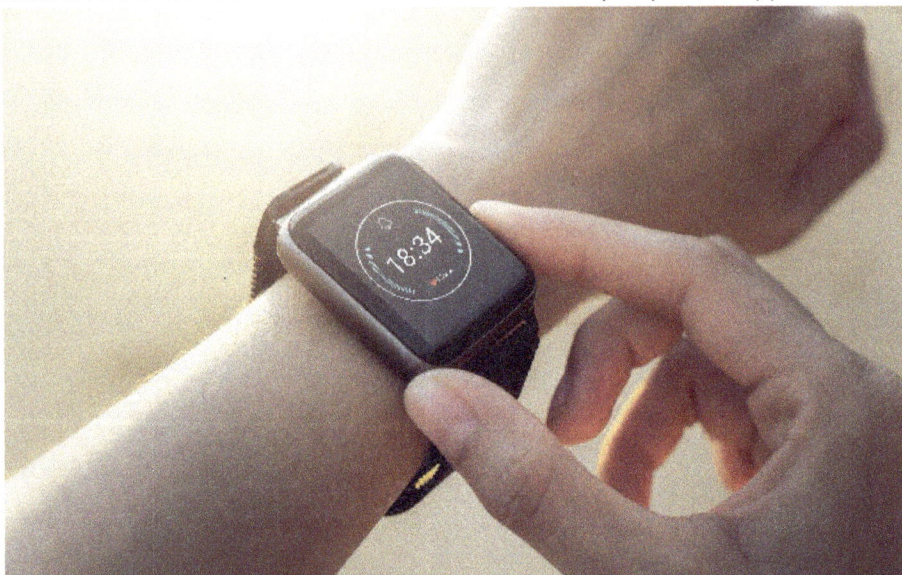

There will be plenty of other job openings and it will never be too late to change.

In fact, repeating *it's too late* to yourself only shuts your brain down and prevents your eyes from seeing the world clearly. By contrast, if your mantra is "it's never too late," you'll become enthusiastic and involved in the game of solving whatever riddle life throws you, while maintaining your focus in a clear, optimistic way.

Much like late merging in traffic, when we wait for the perfect opportunity, we are able to step into the future we always wanted for ourselves.

Waiting for the opening

As you repeat *it's never too late* to yourself and any passengers as you prepare to merge into the exit lane, remain calm and patient. If your lane is brisk and you see no openings early on, this is not an indication that one won't open the closer you get. So, you shouldn't worry. You simply need to wait for it.

There's no need to panic or brake more often than you care to. This level of patience in all things makes life easier and less stressful. Problems may come up at the last moment, but they can all be overcome.

Benjamin Libet, a world-renowned neuroscientist and physiology professor at University of California, San Francisco, studied how delays in our decision-making, even those requiring instantaneous judgments, can be heightened by waiting until the very last moment.[10] Use the following steps to help you through your evaluation:

1. **Determine how long you have**. Even though you know that you need to decide, don't rush. Figure out how long you have. You'll find this can calm your nerves.

2. **Weigh the outcomes**. Use the intervening time to weigh the possible outcomes. Which choice seems the best for you at that moment?

3. **Repeat**. Repeat the process a few times until you lean in a specific direction.

4. **Decide**. At the last possible moment, make your decision.

Libet applied his evaluation to high-speed racing where drivers are at top speeds making decisions. The longer they waited, the better their decisions. This approach works in other areas, such as dating, conversation, how we work, and how we make judgments in general.[11]

Planning seldom works

One simple takeaway from the success of late merging is the fact that most of our plans are subject to interruptions, unexpected changes, new events, postponements, and a whole list of unknown consequences. It's not that we shouldn't plan at all—planning is a healthy activity. It's that our  plans, whether they are for the day or week or next year, are not cast in concrete. Reality fluctuates beyond our control.

A good example is the way we take road trips. Now it's all well and good to make reservations at hotels, restaurants, national parks, and museums along the way. But so much can go wrong. The attractions you scheduled may be too crowded or not worth your time. The hotels may be in poor condition. In fact, you may pass by a point of interest that you can visit only if you cancel one of your reservations. There will always be hotels and restaurants along the way that don't need this level of forethought. And in many cases, the ones that you can't make reservations for, or that you stumbled into, are by far the best. The delights on a road trip are not that you check all the boxes, but rather that it is an adventure that makes you giddy with anticipation. That's a top-tier road trip.

Planning should be like a quick sketch of a portrait. It's not final, a lot can change in the interim, but it serves a purpose of fleshing out an idea for the future. Since the future is unpredictable, we shouldn't spend too much of our time refining these plans. They may work out a certain way, but often a spontaneous event completely unseats our plan or significantly changes it. No need to fret. Keep planning with the spirit that your plan is a rough cut of what's to come.

Going the wrong way happens

We are under the impression that if we stick to a plan and keep our focus, we will succeed. In general, this is well-intentioned. But the simple fact is we live in a world that is hard to predict: even the small things in our lives can go haywire. If we spend our time trying to make sure everything is in order, that every moment is optimal, we fail to see that stepping into a pile of doodoo can be a life-affirming action. Sure, you're reaching for the nearest garden hose, but your world has woken up.

The first step in a life of late merging is accepting the basic truth that you might be going the wrong way. What does this mean? It means that what you thought you wanted was nowhere close. Maybe it was outdated, or that you yourself changed since the last time you thought you knew. Whatever the reason, when you realize you are heading the wrong way, you can't just throw yourself into reverse. You must first figure out where you really want to go.

- **Slow down.** Instead of a complete stop, slow down to let your thoughts bubble to the surface. Try to understand what you are feeling.
- **Strike up a conversation.** Find a friend or stranger with whom you can express your doubts. Remember: you may in fact be on the right path, so first bounce your concerns off someone else. A stranger is much better than a friend since they have no allegiance to your current path.
- **Let major reversals sit for a while.** Don't make any rash decisions if it means a complete reversal. Let your thoughts marinate.

Don't beat yourself up because you had it all planned out and found yourself heading for a proverbial brick wall. Things happen. It's been a fun ride and there's more ahead to enjoy.

Deciding at the last moment

There are many decisions that we find ourselves needing to make during our daily lives. These may be as simple as what to have for breakfast or which shirt or blouse to wear to work. We may find ourselves inundated from morning until night with decisions that we are forced to make one way or another. If you don't make the time, you can end up hungry or wearing your PJs to work.

But we shouldn't be afraid of making decisions. And there's no need to make them in advance. Do you line up your cereal the night before? Do you lay out the clothes you're going to wear the night before? Many do. But spontaneous decisions, those made on the fly, work out to be much better than those pondered again and again.

This also applies to major decisions. What career do you want to have? Which company do you want to work for? Who do you want to marry or partner up with for the rest of your life? Our ability to make these types of decisions is based on our accumulated knowledge and intuition. Malcolm Gladwell explores our ability to do just that in his book *Blink*.[12] The notion that we must study situations for long periods of time and do extensive analyses is shot down. We know more than we realize, and, with the proper frame of mind, we can undertake even the most complicated decisions at the last moment. Late merging helps us to develop these skills as we are constantly challenged to move ahead in varying situations.

By practicing the art of late merging, you are refining your ability to make quick and correct decisions.

Smiling when you're wrong

When you find yourself in conversations on a topic but realize after a while that you were totally wrong in your opinion or your understanding of the facts, what do you do? Do you just keep quiet and look out of place? Do you try to back-pedal your opinion which you so fiercely defended moments earlier?

In many cases, the best thing to do is just smile and enjoy the conversation. Realize that you don't have to be the center of attention to enjoy the banter. You can be on the sidelines, a cup of coffee in hand, listening with a nod and a smile.

Should someone want to pull you back into the conversation by attacking your position, you can easily admire their enthusiasm and recognize how they are tricking you to lose face. Don't fall for it. Continue your smile and say little. You may want to say "interesting" or "yes, that's possible." But don't give in yet; let the conversation move to a different topic or even introduce a new topic different from the one you've stepped into.

You can always excuse yourself for a refill, the use of the facilities, or pretend you need to step away for a call. The goal is to let yourself off the hook. You have no obligation to admit your poor judgment or your poor recall of the facts. You're only human. Just move on.

Spontaneous meetups

When you have a life well-planned, with engagements carefully placed on your calendar, there may be little time for your casual acquaintances. In a life full of late merging, spontaneous meetups are a wonderful way to spend time with people that you've lost contact with. Keep in mind that not everybody is a close friend to whom you can confess your deeply held mistakes and issues. There is a whole network of acquaintances that you run into, or colleagues that you see in the office kitchen. Why not get to know them a little better?

It's easily done when you adopt a flexible schedule, one with fewer planned events.

Instead of a casual hello, reminisce about the last time you ran into one another. Try to recall their interests or the events that brought you together in the past. Talk briefly about events in your life since that time. You can talk about family or work. Then ask about what they have been up to. In other words, start a conversation. Listen to what they have to say. If the possibility of getting together seems real, suggest getting together another time, maybe over coffee. If there is a good connection, exchange contact info. You can simply text your phone number with your name. In the interim, firm up the date and time and suggest something casual. Don't make it too complicated. Just arrange a time to catch up. When the day arrives, send a quick email or text to confirm. Then simply show up.

This keeps your meetups very casual and explores new encounters. In the world of late merging, there is always room.

Last-Minute meals

You may find yourself trying to figure out what to have for dinner or lunch.

If it's only you, it shouldn't be a big deal. But when you add your spouse or partner into the equation, you need to brainstorm what types of meals make sense.

A few factors are involved in this joint decision:

• What type of meal did you both have in mind?
• How hungry are you?
• How much time will it take to prepare the meal?
• What amount of cleanup can you both handle?

The advantage of a last-minute meal is that you tap into your current appetite and what you are truly longing for.

If you prepared a casserole in advance, but don't feel like one now, then this meal would not be as appetizing. The same is true of dishes that you generally like. Leaving meals to the last moment captures what you truly would enjoy. The downside is that you may be absolutely starving with nothing ready to eat.

Don't worry. You can wait a bit longer. The key to last-minute meals is to share the type of food you have in mind and come up with a short list, e.g., Italian *vs* Mexican food. Single out those that can be made or picked up easily. Then simply jump into this last-minute prep. You'll find that meals made this way will land squarely on exactly what you wanted to eat in the first place.

The double-click method of decision-making

We are taught throughout school to analyze situations, logically breaking out the pros and cons before making important decisions. The science behind how well our unconscious minds can come to clear decisions has been tested in a number of situations. The technique, many times referred to as *thin slicing*, finds important patterns in the situations we experience.[13] Late merging trains your unconscious mind to make quick decisions.

As our decisions become more important and their outcomes less reversible, we can still use our intuition to support the direction we take. Instead of deciding once, try doing it twice. That is, the first time, quickly make your decision. Hold onto that thought but don't take any immediate action. Then wait until another time when you can decide all over again.

This process is called the *double-click method*. The decision clicked the first time when it came up, and, more importantly, it was reinforced the second time when the same direction was indicated. Of course, if the second time yielded different results, it would be an indication to table the decision (if you can) until another time.

For example,

- **Ordering Dinner.** In fancy restaurants you may find yourself steeped in indecision. There are so many dishes to choose from, which one should you choose? Many times, we order what we always have ordered, the gazpacho or cioppino. But is it the best decision? Why not explore new dishes instead of re-reading the menu as the waiter visits your table a third time? Use the double-click method to figure out what you want. Pick the top two choices and ask yourself which one you want to have this evening, then ask yourself again. It's better if you do not ask these questions aloud, as it may decrease your standing with your guests.

- **Shopping.** As we walk down the store aisles (either in person or virtually) we are often presented with items that we think we really want, maybe even need. We put them into our shopping cart but feel a sense of ambiguity. Do we really need a safari hat? We've always wanted to go on one, so this might nudge us in the right direction. Or do we really want two tubs of chocolate peanut butter cups? After all, we just swore to ourselves to quit these delicious snacks. Why are the tubs in our shopping cart? This is the perfect time to ask yourself if you should buy the tubs. If your subconscious has a voice, you may find an emphatic *no* as the answer. Hold onto the answer and find a time before checkout to ask again. You may be surprised how well your subconscious understands you and guides you in the right direction.
- **Changing Jobs.** Maybe you've had it with your work or supervisor, and you need a new job. This can be a big decision in your life, since you have friends at work, and you enjoy many things about it. But the time might be right to step off and find a better position. Instead of fussing around with the pros and cons, just look at yourself in the mirror and ask yourself, *should I look around for a better company?* Wait for your inner self to answer. Ignore any traffic around you especially if you've decided to ask yourself the question in the company bathroom. If you get an enthusiastic yes, then hold onto that. Find another time to re-ask yourself. Enthusiastic, solid answers are ones you can count on.
- **Choosing Your Spouse/Partner.** When you have been with a person on different occasions, and you find yourself totally immersed in what they are saying, including the occasional bad joke, they seem to be the right person for you. But how do you make that decision? Granted the other person must feel the same way. The double-click method can work wonders in this situation. Ask yourself if this is *the one*. If you answer an overwhelming yes, then hold off for a bit. Ask yourself on another wholly different occasion the same question. Maybe after the two of you have locked horns over some silly topic. If both times it is an enthusiastic yes, then this person is the one. If it is a sort-of yes, or if you still sense doubts, then hold off. Continue to enjoy their company but wait until another time to ask yourself the question. Maybe rephrase it for clarity.

The way we make decisions has a big impact on our lives. Many of us avoid making them, but at a certain juncture, it is impossible to escape. Driving the freeways in our daily lives can refine these abilities by allowing our subconscious to guide us in our merging activities.

Last-minute fashion

If late merging has taught us anything, it is to rely on our last-minute picks. The day before you might have picked your best outfit for an occasion, but minutes before you head out, you realize that you are setting yourself up for disappointment. Little by little, it seeps in that no one will be noticing you -- except maybe the checkout clerk. The shoes are not that comfortable, and you'll overheat in the heavy coat. And why you chose a headband that you've never worn before but felt like it fit—that's the real puzzler.

For occasions where you are considering something other than your pajamas, you can decide on the spur of the moment. Although pajamas as chic streetwear is really having a moment. But some tips:

- **Don't worry about what you'll wear.** As important as we think it is, it's not. Our friends, coworkers, and others recognize us for who we are. Our conversation and our ability to listen to others at the table is key. What we wear does not matter.
- **Pick something at the last moment.** With its importance diminished, pick the first thing that pops into your head. Whatever it is, just go with it.
- **Don't spend too much time in front of the mirror.** Don't cast doubt on your choices. Make sure you have your keys, wallet, purse, and other sundry items before you leave. Glance briefly in the mirror then head out.

Too often we focus on appearances and not enough on the important parts of getting together with others: the camaraderie, the conversation, and the pure enjoyment of friends. Regardless of how you're dressed, when you show up at events, immerse yourself and get involved.

Ad-libbing

We often feel that we must be prepared for conversations with others who might know more than us on a given subject. Or that we might need to stick to a script if we are presenting to others at work or on a social occasion. But nothing could be further from the truth.

These days being contemporaneous is highly regarded. Anyone who repeats a story they have told *ad naseum* or who appears to read from note cards is considered out of touch. It may sound smooth and make accurate references, but for those listening, it sounds too rehearsed. The top actors are consummate ad-libbers. So many of the scenes we think have been well-scripted and rehearsed are actually spontaneous. Characters' reactions in these scenes feel real and are engaging.

Why? Because they are believable.

When you rely on notes you've jotted down on your phone, you lose creditability. You may seem more fake than usual. So just let go and ad-lib. You may make mistakes, misquote people, misuse references, and fail to find any foundation to what you are saying, but it is authentically you. And that is what your audience, informal or otherwise, wants to hear.

Go for the real you, not perfection. Don't shield yourself from potential mistakes, lapses in memory, drifting and losing the points you were trying to make. We get it. It's *you* we really want to talk with, not some construction that you've labored hard to put in front of us.

Cramming for exams

When we have plenty of time to study, we do not have the pressure to learn. We can stroll through our notes or reread important passages. We can practice writing answers to questions or listening to ourselves regurgitate the facts.

How boring.

We make so little progress memorizing the critical elements of a subject when we are given the time to do so. We idly wander through our subjects, taking breaks to check our email or text friends. But there is little pressure to dive deep. Hours fly by and we're still looking at the same page.

Cramming solves the basic dilemma of pressure. It adds a time constraint that forces you to get to it.   Imagine a game show like *Jeopardy* or *Wheel of Fortune* if there were no time constraints. The participants would just idle away and forget to answer. Placing time constraints enhances our ability to memorize key elements and let less crucial information fall away.   Suddenly our subconscious kicks in with its ability to distinguish what items the test will cover. It gathers this from what your teachers have said, how they have approached certain topics, or emphasized certain points. These probably have gone right past you, especially if you are working on your homework for another class.

Cramming can certainly supplement ongoing studies. But importantly, late merging, it can keep you focused on what's ahead.

Learning to let go

When you are dangling at the end of a rope far above a rocky ravine, the last thing you contemplate is letting go. Yet so much of Zen Buddhism hinges on our ability to let go of ourselves—of our egos, longings, disappointments, sense of self, and our individuality—and blend into the magnificence of the world around us.

This is all well and good, but on a busy freeway, the concept of letting go takes on new dimensions. It's no longer a matter of blending into or connecting to the cosmos. This is a lapse of focus. You're driving on a street, not wafting through the cosmos. The cosmos is not going to steer you to safety or farther up the line. It's all in your hands and letting go in this context does not mean letting go of the steering wheel.

But in daily life when we miss our turn, miss our exit, or fail to meet our own expectations, letting go means just that: forget *about it*. Move on. There's a new challenge around the corner and if you don't have both hands on your internal wheel, you're going to pass it by. That would be just one more thing to chalk up as a disappointment.

As we let these minor failures add up, they create their own roadblocks inside us. Soon, we feel at a loss to attempt anything. We have a line of failures we see as a slowdown ahead that we can do little about. They've already happened. No amount of maneuvering will erase them, no steering will pass them by.

Instead, we must take each minor scratch and scrape in our lives, roll down our proverbial window, and whisk them away. Let them litter someone else's memory. When you are finished, roll up your window and drive on. This may also happen on the freeway when you fail to make a late merge. The exit is gone. You found no gaps to move into. What do you do? Again, let it go. Another exit is not that far away. Keep chipper and move on.

Being at ease when everything is up in the air

When we recognize that change is afoot, we should not be overly worried. Things will work out.

This doesn't mean that we do nothing. But it does mean we stay alert to the next important step. This can be as simple as keeping an eye out for new jobs and careers even if you are satisfied with

where you are. Or it may be attending to small fissures in friendships and relationships before they become larger gaps.

This focus is the same as keeping an eye on gaps in lanes. These can prove to be opportune at the right time. It is this eye to the future, in lanes on either side and certainly in the line ahead, that gives you the heads-up that you can make a move soon.

When you find the opening after keeping an eye on it for a while, simply move in. When everything is up in the air, it is a good reminder that you have the skill set to make it all come together. You should feel calm and energized, alive with new opportunities, and ready for the next step.

Early merging can be a waste of time

Of course, not all early merging is a waste of time. But when it occupies most of your efforts, you may be spending too much time on the details that can shift around. Broad plans, like knowing where to exit on the freeway, are givens. We all need these. But once in place, let some of the details shake themselves out based on how events unfold. Make mental notes on the details and allow them to shift in your head. Focus on the present. If you are driving, it is an easy reminder since you'll see cars moving in and out of your flow.

But in real life, our minds can fixate on minute details. It's like an artist planning every stroke to use in a painting: why plan at this level when you can just paint when the time comes? It's like getting into our Halloween costumes and practicing our trick-or-treat routes in the middle of the summer.

Early merging has some benefits in laying out broad goals and plans. These goals can be reminders of new directions you want to take, at work, in your relationships or in life itself. Take some small steps so you can better learn if these goals are worth pursuing. In this way you can see if you have the skills you need to move forward.

Arriving late is trendy

One of the side effects of deciding at the last moment is that you cram a lot of living into a limited amount of time. The average person in the U.S. lives 76 years. If your average time in lines is decreased, you'll effectively live longer. If 25% of your professional and school life can be saved by not waiting in lines, you're effectively living another 12.5 years. Not in a quantitative way *per se*, but in experiencing all that life can be. If you really think about it, tailoring your activities so that you arrive early is simply a poor use of your time.

Instead, arriving five or ten minutes late is usually not a big deal. In Japan of course, this is considered an insult to your host. But in the U.S. and other countries, this is considered par for the course. So, if your spouse is merging early on getting ready for an event, that means you can relax and enjoy a few extra minutes of other activities. If you are deciding on what to wear or contemplating other important issues on your phone, take your time. The skills developed by late merging on the freeway apply to gauging the time needed to get ready for the event.

Arrive late with apologies and engage your friends and acquaintances with your recent late merge experiences. They will get a better understanding of your point of view. And it may help them to arrive a bit later themselves. In the end, it will only encourage a greater sense of camaraderie.

Rushing does not need be so frantic

When you find yourself rushing around and cleaning up the mess you've made before friends arrive, stop for a moment. Realize that really, it's not that important. If it's because you need to make it to an appointment on time, then relax. Your appointments will be fine. Usually, the office that makes your appointment has already taken into account late arrivals or when the schedules get elongated due to extended time needed.

If you are hurrying around for a restaurant reservation that has strict policies about being late, call them and explain your situation. They will usually hold the table for you. There's no need to panic. That just makes your evening get off to a bad start.

If you are meeting friends or on a date, a quick text should do the trick.

Now take a deep breath and relax. You can keep your agility in getting ready or organizing, just not in the frantic mode you switch into. There are times when we must move quickly, and certainly merging on the freeway is one of them. But your mood should be carefree.

In fact, your friends and family will appreciate your calmness as you move effortlessly around, collecting items you need, getting ready, and changing outfits as the event dictates.

Reading by skipping ahead

Maybe you're a person who never finishes the books you start. It's the trend these days. Maybe the books on your bedside table never get touched. Or maybe they gather dust because you are exhausted by the end of the day, and you end up scrolling on your phone instead of reading.

Part of the problem is your approach to reading. You open the cover and begin at the beginning. A few minutes in and you wish the author would pick up the pace. You just want to get to the exciting part, so why isn't it in the first chapters? For nonfiction books, there may be so many facts thrown at you that you simply lose interest. These days it's easier to watch a YouTube video.

The real problem is that you are reading the old-fashioned way. You are reading every word on every line, start to finish, and left to right. If this is assigned reading, you are probably trying to be careful that you don't overlook details that might be on the final exam. But even here, approach is everything.

Instead of getting in line, paragraph-by-paragraph, chapter-by-chapter, jump around and jump ahead.

- **Peruse the opening.** Start at the beginning of the book and search for the main topic to be covered. You'll find examples and summations that can help you get your arms around the main goals of the author.

- **Check out the table of contents.** Go back to the Contents page to get an idea of how the author is planning to lay out the topics. All the chapters fit under their overarching goal. Whatever point the author is trying to make can usually be found in the chapter titles.
- **Jump between chapters.** Don't worry about following the flow of the book. Instead jump around to the chapters that you find the most interesting. Read the opening and closing paragraphs, then make a mental note of interesting sentences in the chapter.
- **Jot down notes.** With a piece of paper handy or in the margins, jot down your thoughts and any detail you want to hold onto.
- **Reread sections.** When you find yourself confused, don't worry. You'll get the hang of the book. Circle back another time and reread the chapters you enjoyed, and the ones that caused you any confusion.

For novels, you can use the same approach, although you'll be fast-forwarding the timeline. You'll see the main characters take on certain actions and hear them talk. This can be fun, especially if you read their transformations out of order. When a work of fiction has too many characters to remember, the author may be trying to show you how main characters' actions affected the minor characters, and *vice versa*. That's all well and good but keep your focus on the main characters. You can always go back and revisit the chapters.

In many ways, reading a book out of order is like solving a puzzle. You'll get a sense of where the book is going and try to assemble the various paragraphs in some order to make sense out of them. This approach ends up making reading a lot more fun.

Switching topics in conversations

If you are with a group and a lively discussion is underway, you may feel that you should contribute to the topic.   For example, if a public figure makes a statement on the news, or certain headlines generate a lot of talk, you may find your group splitting into two camps: one will support the

direction of the statement or news, and the other will push back against it. You may find yourself nonplussed by the topic. Maybe it's been overly discussed, even by the same group. Or it makes little difference since there is little anyone in the group can do about it but talk. It can be a waste of time. Talk, as they say, is cheap.

There's no need to get overly invested in your point of view. While you may want to support your friends, perhaps you understand the merits of both sides. Instead of picking a side or trying to act as mediator to clarify positions the group is taking, the best way to proceed is simply to change topics.

This may sound like you don't really think the topic is important, or that you think your friends are wrong. But in fact, you simply have a subject that came to mind, and you introduce it in a light and cheerful way. For example, instead of politics, maybe you want to ask your friends if they watched the latest episode of *American Ninja Warrior*. The last few contestants nailed that vertical wall! Introduce the new topic by saying *not to change the topic…*

You may see your friends gulp their drinks in hand. Yes, they may be startled by your perceived lack of attention. But you are also making a statement: *Let's move on*. If you get no response, then describe your favorite part.

Changing subjects in the middle of a conversation is usually done by those who have the *chutzpah* to do so.

Ignore directions meant mostly for others

You may remember your first-grade class when your teacher gave you directions on what not to do. For example, don't run in the hallways. Or, in the reading circles, don't jump up and down when you know the answer. In most cases, instructions like these are easy to follow and don't create any issues.

But occasionally you may find that directions that you are given don't make sense or seriously inhibit an important action you want to take. If we were to follow every direction we're given, we'd find our lives boring, and our opportunities quite limited.

In much the same way we are told not to late merge in traffic, many of these instructions are overdone. When considering whether to ignore directions, keep in mind the following:

- Does stepping over the line hurt or harm anyone? If not, then there is more reason to question why the instructions must be followed.
- If everyone failed to follow the rules, would it cause major issues? Even here, you're the only one that may be considering the break. If others follow, then it is a test of whether the instruction was too restrictive.
- Is there a good reason for the rule? If it's not clear, then consider stepping over the line.

It is always important to understand why the directions we are given. If these are for the better good, it is understandable. If they are to prevent harm to others, we should respect them. But in other cases, you may find yourself needing to step over the line to explore new possibilities or to help others. In these cases, it is best to sidestep the directions if you feel it can open up a new opportunity.

Making friends by jumping ahead

These days you may find you spend more time by yourself. And when you need to connect, it's in a Zoom meeting or posting on social media. This puts a lot of distance between you and the people you want to hang out with.

We never know who will wind up a friend, someone we can confide in, tell the stories we are least proud of, and be considered a confidant of their stories in return. Many times, you may find yourself on the periphery, more an associate or bystander than a friend.

When this occurs, it is largely because you stand in line and wait your turn for the right occasion. This is understandable, and you may have been taught your manners by your parents who wanted you to be courteous and not too forward. You may think of yourself as more of an introvert, afraid to express yourself lest someone beat you down with some fact that blows a topic of interest.

The solution is to step to the front and interact with others to express who you are and your emotions around recent or current events. You may think that you must start at the end of the line of casual conversation (e.g., the weather), before working your way to meatier topics.

Instead, press the *skip* button in conversation. Forget the long line of topics and interactions that lead to a more involved interaction. Blurt out whatever is on your mind from experiences over the last few days. Ignore the gasps from others. Ask for advice or confide in things of importance with people you run into. The downside is that your life, which you may have kept closer to the vest, is now out in the open. To be clear, this does not mean getting too intimate with strangers about your life.

For example, don't discuss your recent urinary tract infection with your coworker by the water cooler, or your upcoming dermatologist appointment for a weird skin thing in the grocery checkout line. Instead start with events that have made you happy. This can be leveling up in a game or connecting with a relative. And while you're at it, think about making your relatives your friends. Sure, your sibling continually threw a bunch of insults in your direction when you were younger. Put these in your memory trash bin and give them a call to catch up.

It is important once you start your interaction to listen to the other person. Listening is much like finding gaps in lines: there are subtle indications of where the other person is at. You can pick upon cues to ask courteous questions.

Making friends in the old-fashioned way takes time. With a late-merging approach, you jump ahead of the usual topics and begin revealing more about yourself and being curious about the other person. Don't try to gauge how well you do. Just keep doing it and new friendships will sprout around you.

8. Quick Guide

Whether you are commuting each day or interacting with friends face-to-face, try making decisions more spontaneously. Use a late merge mindset and you'll find life can be more exciting and fulfilling.

1. Avoid lines wherever possible

Although our natural inclination is to get into lines when we see them, avoid them wherever possible. It means finding times when there are no lines, courteously moving to the front using the skills outlined in this book.

2. Don't rush to decide

You'll have more information by waiting until the last moment to make decisions. It does not hurt to research the important factors involved. But it is not necessary to plan everything in minute detail.

3. Learn to let go

Whether it's past decisions or old relationships that you keep pondering, learn to let go and focus on the present. This may sound very Zen-like, and it is. It allows you to focus on what's happening now and have a clear head when the time comes to act.

4. Find the openings

On the road and in your daily life, find the openings. These may be spaces in the lanes when you are stuck in traffic. Or they may be areas at work and in your daily life where something is missing.

5. Fill the openings

When you find an opening, simply fill it. On the road, this is late merging and is done courteously. It will speed up your daily commutes. In real life, these may be with your own ideas and actions. Take the initiative when you recognize that something's missing or lagging.

6. Jump ahead

When you sense the direction in conversations, simply jump ahead to the conclusions. Why wait for discussions to chew over what is pretty much decided? In the routines of life, recognize where things are going, and get a head start. If it is your job that is lacking, jump ahead to changing it. If it is a relationship that you recognize is fulfilling, move forward to making it last.

7. Be modest

No one likes someone who is always bragging, casting themselves as the hero of their stories. Don't fall into the trap of flaunting your successes. Instead, recognize others in their quest to live full lives.

8. Take time to enjoy

Instead of waiting for those moments you plan to enjoy, relish them as they happen. Don't move onto the next thing until you've embraced where you're at. Give yourself permission to indulge your senses in the beauty of the moment.

9. Glossary

The following is a list of terms used frequently by late mergers.

Term	Meaning
Cram	To study when there is little time left, or to move into a lane where the space is a little too small
Crossover	The act of changing multiple lanes quickly across a freeway
Disciplined Driving Demeanor (DDD)	A mindset that continually focuses on the road and surroundings
Double-click	A way to make decisions quickly by waiting for the intuitive second consideration
Driver	The person behind the wheel
Dummy	A person who momentarily lacks the mental skills to drive properly or gets easily distracted
Early Merge	Getting in line way too soon
Exit	The ultimate destination on a freeway and goal of a late merge
Fast lanes	The lanes on a freeway that move the quickest, not always the ones on the left
Flow	The natural rhythm on a freeway
Gap	The space between two cars when a driver lags
Gulp	The act of drinking liquids in the car too quickly
Honk	To use the horn
Lag	The act when a driver fails to keep up with the car in front of them in a line
Line	A physical conundrum of cars or people waiting one behind another, best avoided
Merge	The act of changing lanes

Term	Meaning
One-handed	A driving style that requires only one hand to steer a car
Pre-Merge	Getting ready to merge by moving next to a gap
Sandwiching	The act of enclosing another car in their position, providing little leeway for them to move; also, preparing a one-handed meal between two slices of bread
Shushing	The act of a driver of telling passengers to keep the noise level down
Signaling	When a driver who lets the car behind them know what they are up to
Slowpoke	A driver who backs up their lane by driving too slowly
Spurting	Speeding up then slowing down
Stupid driving	Usually done by dummies, driving erratically
Toot	A brief honk or, in some cases, a warning to passengers in your vehicle
Zigzag	The act of moving back and forth between lanes to move ahead
Zipper merge	Merging when two lanes converge to a single lane
Zonked	Feeling tired

10. Endnotes

[1] CalTrans. https://dot.ca.gov/programs/traffic-operations/census

[2] *Evaluation Of a Dynamic Late Merge System*, Minnesota Department of Transportation, 2003.

[3] *Traffic: Why We Drive the Way We Do,* Alfred Knopf, New York, 2008, p. 4.

[4] Rogers, Martin. *Highway Engineering*, Blackwell Publishing, 2003. p.73.

[5] *Highway Capacity Manual.* Special Report 209. Transportation Research Board. Washington, D.C., 1985.

[6] Menand, Louis. *The Metaphysical Club: A Story of Ideas in America.* Farrar, Straus and Ginoux. New York, 2001. Pp. 337 - 362.

[7] Farman, Jason. *Delayed Response: The Art of Waiting from the Ancient to the Instant World*, New Haven: Yale University Press, 2018. https://doi.org/10.12987/9780300240726

[8] *ibid*

[9] Schweizer, Harold. *On Waiting*, Routledge, London. 2008.

[10] Libet, Benjamin. *Mind Time: The Temporal Factor in Consciousness,* Harvard University Press, 2003, pp 109 -111.

[11] Partnoy, Frank. *Wait The Art and Science of Delay*. Public Affairs, New York, 2012.

[12] Gladwell, Malcolm. *Blink: The Power of Thinking Without Thinking*, Little, Brown & Company, New York, 2005.

[13] Gladwell, M., 2005.p. 23.

www.ingramcontent.com/pod-product-compliance
Lightning Source LLC
Chambersburg PA
CBHW061814290426
44110CB00026B/2868